THE PYRAMIDS

John Weeks

GENERAL EDITOR TREVOR CAIRNS

ART EDITORS BANKS AND MILES

CAMBRIDGE
AT THE UNIVERSITY PRESS 1971

Diagrams by Anthony Smith

Illustrations in this volume are reproduced by kind permission of the following:
front cover, Michael Holford; pp. 4 (Pyramid of Zoser), 6, 9, 10, 11 (spearmen and bowmen), 15, 17 (flooded palm groves), 29, 30, 36 (packing blocks on Pyramid of Cheops), 37, Roger-Viollet, Paris; 5 (Pyramid of Dahshur), 45, 48 (Mycerinus and Chamerenebti), Department of Egyptology, University College, London; 8 (uncoffined mummy), 14, back cover, Trustees of the British Museum; 5, 8 (stone sarcophagus), 12 (relief), 13, 48 (Zoser, Cheops, and Chephren), Hirmer Fotoarchiv, Munich; 11 (model of a maidservant), Roger Wood; 11 (wall painting), Egyptian Expedition: Metropolitan Museum of Art, New York; 12 (potter), Oriental Museum, University of Chicago; 16 (papyrus map now in Turin Museum), 20, 21, 24, 25, 28, 32, 36 (casing blocks on Great Pyramid), 44, from Clark & Engelbach, *Ancient Egyptian Masonry*, Oxford 1930, the Clarendon Press; 17 (cultivated land in the Nile Valley), J. Allan Cash; 33, *Annales du Service des Antiquités*, vol. 38, plate XCIV; the drawings on pp. 40 & 41 from Dr I. E. S. Edwards' *The Pyramids of Egypt*, the author and Penguin Books Ltd.

Note on illustrations. Many of the pictures in this book are photographs of models, carvings or paintings that have been found in ancient Egyptian tombs. When no date is given the object comes from the centuries during which the pyramids were being built. Evidence from later periods is dated. Diagrams throughout the book are not necessarily to scale.

front cover
The pyramids of Chephren and Cheops at Giza.
Cheops' Pyramid (right), or the Great Pyramid, was the largest and best designed of them all. When new, Chephren's Pyramid, now $447\frac{1}{2}$ feet high, was 471 feet high, 10 feet shorter than Cheops' Pyramid. Now it is $2\frac{1}{2}$ feet shorter, but standing on higher ground than its neighbour, gives the impression of being slightly taller.

back cover
A painted wooden model of a funerary boat probably carved during the Middle Kingdom about 2000 BC. The figures at the prow and stern represent the goddesses Isis and Nephthys; a priest reads spells over the mummy from a papyrus scroll; by the prow is an altar. At the funeral a real boat would have been towed.

Published by the Syndics of the Cambridge University Press
Bentley House, 200 Euston Road, London, NW1 2DB
American Branch: 32 East 57th Street, New York, N.Y.10022

© Cambridge University Press 1971

Library of Congress Catalogue Card Number: 74–111135
ISBN 0 521 07240 9

First published 1971
Reprinted 1972

Type-set by Hazell, Watson and Viney
Printed and bound in Great Britain
by Jarrold and Sons Ltd, Norwich

The author and publishers acknowledge with gratitude their debt to the work of Dr I. E. S. Edwards contained in his book *The Pyramids of Egypt* published by Penguin Books Ltd.

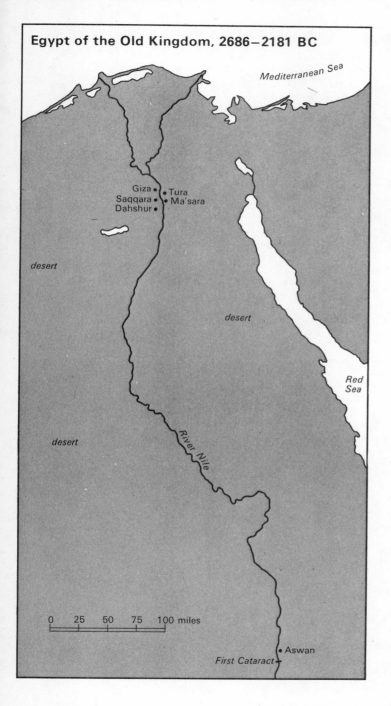

Egypt of the Old Kingdom, 2686–2181 BC

Mediterranean Sea

Giza
Saqqara
Dahshur
Tura
Ma'sara

desert

desert

Red
Sea

desert

River Nile

0   25   50   75   100 miles

Aswan

First Cataract

Contents

The Giza pyramids. The
Great Pyramid of Cheops
(far right), and the
pyramids of Chephren
(centre) and Mycerinus.

The Step Pyramid,
Saqqara.

4

The Bent Pyramid of Dahshur. Externally it is the best preserved of all the pyramids.

The Great Pyramid with the Sphinx in the foreground. The Sphinx was carved in Chephren's reign from a knoll of rock.

1. LAND OF THE PYRAMIDS

The oldest stone buildings in the world are the pyramids. They have stood for nearly 5,000 years and it seems likely that they will continue to stand for thousands of years yet. Because they are so huge, strong and old, people have always been fascinated by the pyramids. The aim of this book is to examine why and how the pyramids were built.

Pyramids are not a rarity in Egypt. There are over eighty of them scattered along the banks of the Nile, some of which vary in shape from the true pyramids. The most famous of the strangely shaped pyramids are the 'Step' pyramid and the 'Bent' pyramid. To understand anything about them, we need to know something about the Egypt of about 5,000 years ago when the first and greatest pyramids were built. Life there was very different from life in most of the rest of the world, which was still uncivilized.

The pharaohs of ancient Egypt were the first real kings in the world. That is, they ruled over a complete country rather than a town or a tribe. It was because they were so powerful that they were able to build such tombs as the pyramids. These early kings built the largest pyramids, like the 'Great Pyramid' of the pharaoh Cheops. Later kings had to make do with smaller pyramids or do without a pyramid altogether. Much later in Egyptian history the kings decided that a tomb cut out of solid rock, and hidden from sight, was a safer place than a pyramid to keep a body. The picture opposite shows the 'Valley of the Kings', a desolate, cliff-bound valley which contains the tombs of many later pharaohs.

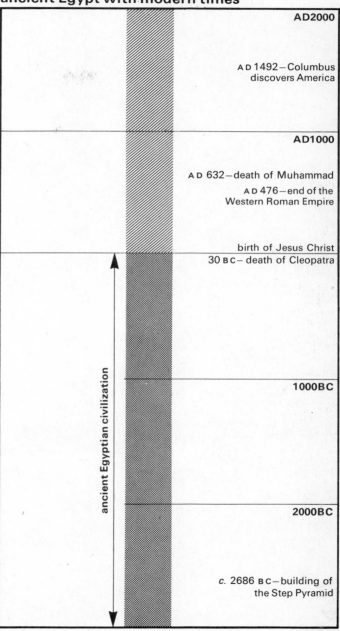

Time chart comparing
ancient Egypt with modern times

AD2000

AD 1492 – Columbus
discovers America

AD1000

AD 632 – death of Muhammad
AD 476 – end of the
Western Roman Empire

birth of Jesus Christ
30 BC – death of Cleopatra

ancient Egyptian civilization

1000BC

2000BC

c. 2686 BC – building of
the Step Pyramid

3000BC

It was tremendously important to an Egyptian that when he died his body should be preserved and protected. Do you wish to see one? All you need to do is go along to any large museum. If you asked the curator he could probably show you a mummy gathering dust in the museum cellars. These dead Egyptians are thousands of years old, yet they are not rare. For example there are sixty mummies on display in the British Museum.

The Egyptians used to preserve their dead in a very special way. Firstly they removed the brain and other organs, except for the heart, from inside the body. The intestines were kept in special sealed jars called 'canopic jars'. Museums also possess many of these jars. The body was then treated for a long time in a substance called natron. This was to preserve it before it was tightly wrapped in linen bandages. The mummy then was placed in a coffin and put into the tomb or pyramid. We know all about the Egyptian views on life after death because the Egyptians explained them in pictorial writings called 'The Book of the Dead'. The ancient Egyptians seem to have been gloomy people, interested only in death. Is this a true picture? To find out let us look at the life of the pharaoh and his people, using the pictures which were painted at that time.

above left: An uncoffined mummy preserved in the dry sands before 3100 BC

left: Stone sarcophagus of Ra'wer. This type of huge outer coffin was placed in the burial chamber before completion of the pyramid.

right: Anubis, the jackal-headed god of embalming *c.* 1100 BC.

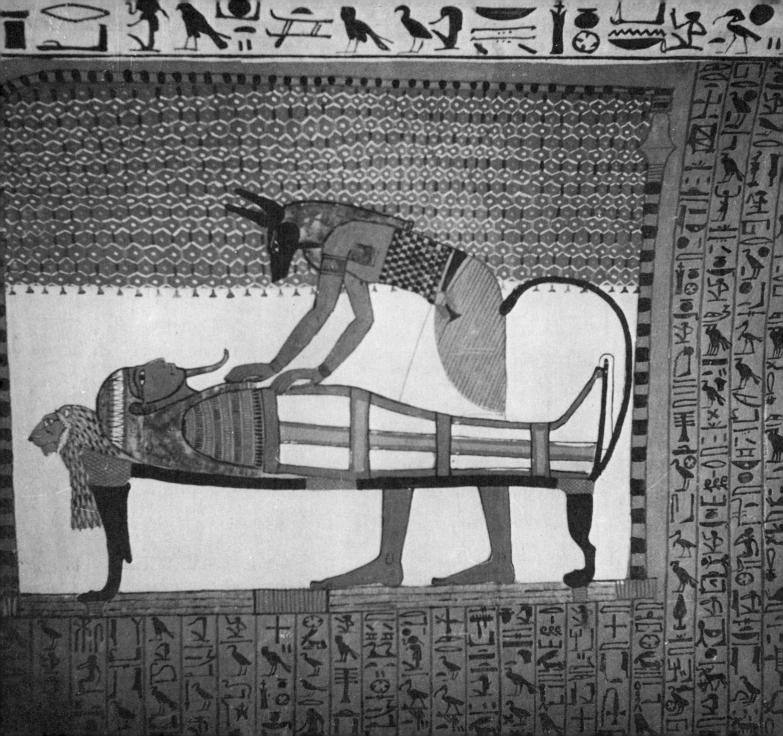

Where to build a pyramid?

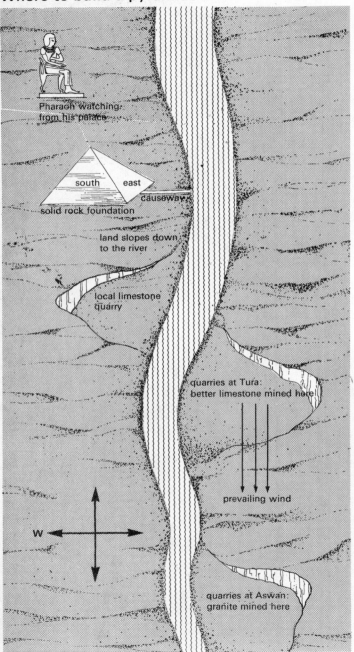

Pharaoh watching
from his palace

south   east

causeway

solid rock foundation

land slopes down
to the river

local limestone
quarry

quarries at Tura:
better limestone mined here

prevailing wind

W

quarries at Aswan:
granite mined here

The only useful part of Egypt is the long, fertile Nile Valley which is flanked by desert. This valley makes very good farming land, and most of the ordinary people were farmers. They had to be very careful farmers as it virtually never rains in Egypt and all water has to come from the Nile. The ancient Egyptians were the first people to irrigate their land by cutting shallow channels in the ground to carry water to otherwise arid land. This knowledge stood them in good stead as we shall see later when discussing the planning of a pyramid. The peasants who could not earn a living from the land probably became soldiers and sailors, or servants to the rich.

Like any civilized people the Egyptians had men who followed skilled occupations. These men would be far fewer in number than the farmers. Some would be skilled workmen such as woodcarvers, stonemasons, metal-workers, builders and shop-keepers. These men would probably carry on the trades of their ancestors.

The river Nile at Aswan.

above: Spearmen and bowmen of the Egyptian army, *c.* 1100 BC.

left: A painted wooden model of a maidservant, *c.* 2000 BC.

right: Harvest scene, *c.* 1500 BC. Note the two girls squabbling, the girl having a thorn drawn from her foot, and the man snoozing beneath a tree.

Limestone statuette of
a potter, *c.* 2200 BC.

Hunting expedition in the papyrus marshes. Note the
great variety of wild life.

Higher grades of occupations, which would be confined to the wealthy families, and which needed a good education, were made up of teachers, architects, and priests and scribes who were also in some cases doctors and astronomers.

The nobles, apart from seeing to the running of their large estates, seemed to have spent most of their time enjoying life. A favourite form of amusement was hunting and fishing in the papyrus marshes which no longer exist naturally in modern Egypt. We can see quite clearly in the picture below how they went about that sport. Notice particularly the flat-topped boat; the girl holding the man's leg whilst he spears fish. The other man is shown flinging his throwing-stick at some birds. The types of game which used to abound in the marshes were hippopotami, hyaenas and geese, so hunting could be very exciting.

Papyrus reeds from these marshes were used for making a form of writing material. Papyrus scrolls were probably read much as we read books today and filled up any spare leisure time. They even had their comics as we can see from the papyrus on the next page.

Fishing and fowling in the papyrus marshes, *c.* 1500 BC.

Papyrus showing beasts of prey looking after and playing with the animals they live on. It is easy enough to see what the cartoonist really meant.

The rich Egyptians enjoyed having large and expensive parties as we can see from the pictures opposite. Parties were probably held quite often in their large, luxurious houses. The noblemen and their wives also liked to dress up in fine clothes, use perfumes, wear wigs, make-up and jewelry to make themselves more attractive.

The pharaoh and his people seem to have been quite normal after all. It is obvious that they could and did enjoy themselves when they had the chance. But it is also true to say that they were more concerned with death than we are today. To be more correct it would be better to say 'life after death' rather than 'death'. The ancient Egyptians believed that 'life after death' was more important than life itself. That is why they prepared for death whilst they were still alive. The pharaoh would often go along to see his pyramid whilst it was being built. As we mentioned on page 7, the pharaoh wanted a safe place for his body when he died. The huge, strong pyramid with its secret rooms and corridors certainly seemed a safe enough place at the time. The body was mummified, because they believed that only if it was preserved could the pharaoh enjoy eternal life. Many articles, as well as food, were buried with the king for him to use in his 'after life'. These were to enable him to live in the same manner as he had done before his death. This meant, amongst other things, to enjoy himself in all the ways he had done when he was alive. The ancient Egyptians did not fear death, and probably accepted it much more readily than we do today. This may have been because they believed that they could ensure eternal life by taking the simple precautions that have already been mentioned.

So we can understand why the king wanted a great, strong tomb. But why was it a pyramid? There have been many theories about the shape of the pyramids. A very practical theory is that it was the easiest way in which to build a large, tall building. We can judge this for ourselves when we read about the actual building of the pyramids. It is true that the pyramid's shape gives it immense strength and the best chance to last 'forever', which is what most concerned the pharaohs. Another theory, based upon one of ancient Egypt's religious cults, is that the pyramid was a ramp representing the rays of the sun upon which the dead kings could climb to heaven. The king would get into the boat carrying a fiery ball which crossed the sky from east to west. During the night the boat would travel from west to east through the underworld. The fiery ball which the boat carried was of course the sun, and its passage an explanation of day and night.

All through the ages people have wondered at the purpose of the pyramids. At times they have been thought treasure-houses, or observatories, or granaries and even means of telling the future. The truth, we can be almost certain, is that they had one main practical purpose: to provide a fitting tomb in which the pharaoh could safeguard his body, and, as a result, his eternal life.

above: Grand ladies,
assisted by a servant girl,
prepare for dinner with
a royal minister,
c. 1425 BC.

Entertainers at the feast.

2. PLANNING THE PYRAMID

The pyramids still stand today and some of them look much as they must have done when they were built thousands of years ago. Most of the damage suffered by the pyramids has been at the hands of men who were looking for treasure, or more often for stone to use in modern buildings. The dry climate of Egypt has helped to preserve the pyramids, and their very shape has made them less likely to fall into ruin. These are good reasons why the pyramids can still be seen today, but perhaps the most important reason is that they were planned to last 'forever'.

There are no writings or pictures to show us how the Egyptians planned and built their pyramids. That plans were made for the building of pyramids is virtually certain because plans of other large works have fortunately been preserved.

We are only able to guess at the methods used, with the help given us by a study of the actual pyramids and the various tools which have been found by archaeologists.

One thing is certain. There must have been months of careful observation and planning before the Egyptians could start to build a pyramid. The first thing they had to do was to choose a suitable place. You may think that this would be easy with miles and miles of empty desert all around them, but a pyramid could not be built anywhere. Certain rules had to be followed.

The pyramid had to be on the west side of the Nile; the side on which the sun set. This was done for religious reasons. The pyramid must stand well above the level of the river to protect it against the regular floods. The pyramid must not be too far from the Nile as the stones to build it would be carried in boats, down the river to the nearest possible point. Water transport was of course much easier than land transport. The builders would have to find a rock base which was not likely to crack under the great weight of the pyramid. Finally the pyramid would have to be near the capital, or better still near to the king's palace so that he could visit it easily and personally check the progress being made on his tomb. Look at the sketch map on page 10.

When the position had been decided on, the builders could get to work on planning the pyramid. First, they would remove the top layer of sand and gravel to get down to the bare rock underneath. This would be the firm foundation of the pyramid. Before they could use the rock as a foundation it had to be made perfectly level. The base of the 'Great Pyramid', each side of which is 755 feet long is almost perfectly level. When we say level we do not include a mound of rock in the middle left by the builders to save time and building materials. The south-east corner is only half an inch higher than the north-west corner. This is a tremendous achievement, considering the great area covered by the base of the pyramid.

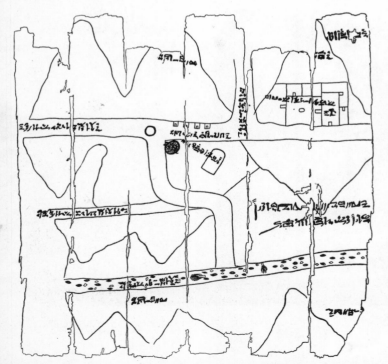

Plan of a gold mine on papyrus, *c.* 1300 BC.

Palm groves flooded by the Nile north of Abu Simbel.

How did they do it? The probable answer is that they used the experience they had gained over many years on crop irrigation. You will remember that the farmers had to cut channels in the ground, to make the best use of the river water to grow more crops. They also had a good calendar which made it possible for them to know when to plant their crops. The Egyptians knew that water finds its own level so they probably used the same method when they wanted to build a pyramid. Look at the picture showing cultivated land on the banks of the Nile.

Flooding a field in the Nile Valley.

Clearing the sand to expose the bare rock

sand

rock

Levelling the site
a. marking out the correct level

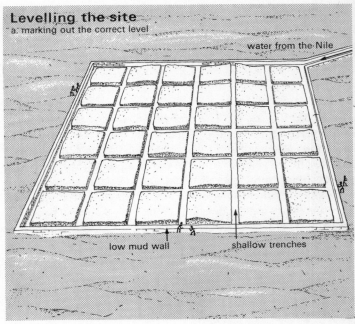

water from the Nile

low mud wall

shallow trenches

Levelling the site
b. cutting away the surplus stone and filling in the holes

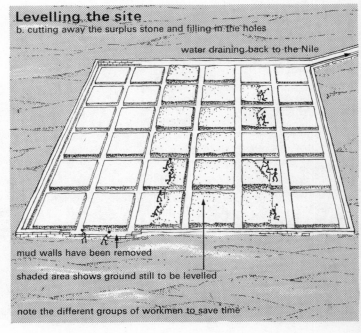

water draining back to the Nile

mud walls have been removed

shaded area shows ground still to be levelled

note the different groups of workmen to save time

The first step would be to build low mud walls around the area to be levelled and cut criss-cross trenches on the floor of the enclosure. Water from the Nile would then be let into the enclosure where it would run along and partly fill the shallow trenches. The workmen would mark the correct level as shown by the water and it would be drained away. Groups of workmen would work on different parts of the base until the whole area around the trenches was level. The trenches would then be filled up with small rocks and rubble to make the whole base perfectly level.

The pyramid could not face in just any direction. Each side had to face one of the four cardinal points. The cardinal points are north, south, east and west. Nearly every child today has seen a magnetic compass and knows how easy it is to calculate any direction. The Egyptians knew nothing of the compass. How then did they find out exactly where these cardinal points lay?

We do not know for certain how the Egyptians estimated the four cardinal points. Their measurements are too accurate to have been gained from a study of the sun or the Pole Star. The main problem seems to have been to draw a line running due north and south.

It is likely that the Egyptians found true north by sighting on a star in the northern sky. They would observe the rising and setting positions of the star and bisect the angle formed by the passage of the star. To do this properly they had to create an artificial horizon because even the smallest rise or dip in the desert would upset their calculations.

To get the necessary accuracy they would build a circular mud wall on the already levelled pyramid site. The man standing at the centre of the area inside the wall should not be able to see over the wall. The wall would not have to be higher than a man could reach, and the whole of its circumference would have to be on a level plane. The top of the wall would provide the required artificial horizon.

The surveyor, standing at the centre of the circle formed by the wall, would look through a cleft stick called a 'bay'. Facing in an easterly direction he would wait until the selected star rose above the wall. The wall would be marked at that spot. Several hours later the star would sink below the wall in a westerly direction and this point would be marked on the wall.

A line would be drawn from each mark on the wall down to the ground. A plumb line would be used to make sure that the line was exactly perpendicular. These lines would be extended to the centre of the circle, and when the angle formed by the lines was bisected it would give a line running due north and south. We know that the ancient Egyptians had instruments for drawing right angles so it would be simple for them to calculate east and west once the north–south line had been drawn.

Finding North by the stars

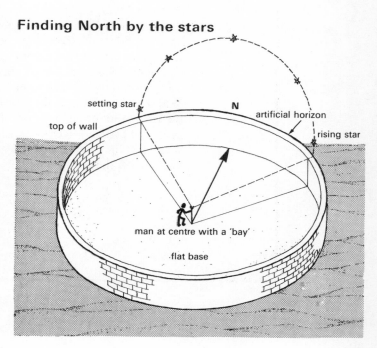

setting star

top of wall

N

artificial horizon

rising star

man at centre with a 'bay'

flat base

The base of the pyramid would have to be in the shape of a perfect square. This meant that all four sides would have to be exactly the same length and all four angles must be right angles. This must have been very difficult, especially as large distances had to be measured. Each side of the 'Great Pyramid' measured about 755 feet in length. This is roughly two-and-a-half times as long as a large football pitch, and the area of the base is about seven-and-a-half times the area of a large football pitch.

The Egyptians did not have metal measuring tapes, but had to make do with measuring cords of palm-fibre or flax-fibre which were liable to stretch when used to measure such great distances. We should not be surprised to find that the builders did not always achieve their perfect square. Even so, there is only slightly less than eight inches difference between the longest and shortest sides of the 'Great Pyramid'.

The base would at last be ready for the builders, but before they could start they had to have the stone with which to build. Whilst the site was being prepared stone was already being quarried and brought down the river to a place near the proposed pyramid. We shall see in the next two chapters, before we look at the actual building of the pyramid, how they quarried and carried those huge amounts of stone.

The base of the Great Pyramid compared to a large football pitch
the base area of the pyramid is equal to the area of 7½ football pitches

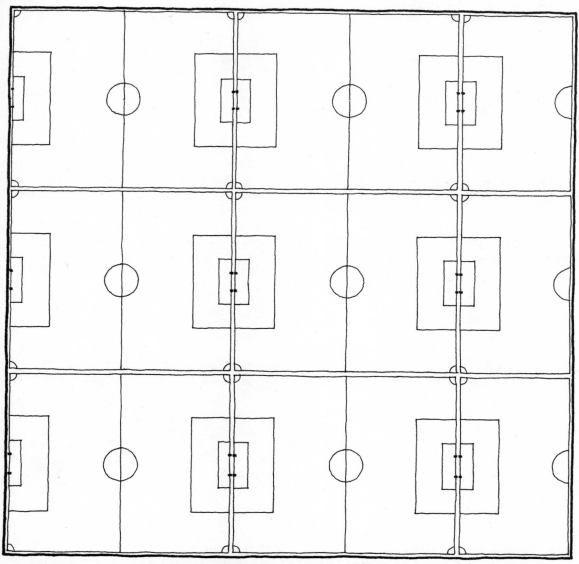

one side of the pyramid is equal to 2½ times the length of a football pitch

3. THE STONES – QUARRYING AND CUTTING

The pyramids were built of two different kinds of rock: a fairly soft rock called limestone which made up most of the pyramid, and a much harder rock called granite which was only used in fairly small quantities. These rocks had to be quarried from the ground, and in Egypt today many of these ancient quarries are still being worked.

Nearly all the quarries which supplied the stone for building the pyramids were close to the banks of the Nile. So were nearly all the pyramids during the period when the Nile overflowed its banks, which probably indicates that the sacred river Nile was also used to carry the stones from the quarries to the places where the pyramids were being built. The limestone quarries were near to the pyramids, whilst the nearest granite quarries were 500 miles away. This is because you usually only find one main type of rock in any one area.

At this stage you may be wondering why the Egyptians did not build their pyramids completely out of granite if they wanted them to last forever. The answer is a very practical one. The granite was farther away than the limestone and more difficult to quarry because of its hardness. So to build a pyramid of granite would be much more difficult and expensive; and, perhaps worst of all from the Egyptians' point of view, it would take far longer to build. The kings wanted to make sure that their bodies had a safe resting place and a suitable monument before they died. They did not want to rely on their successors to finish the pyramid, because they would be much more interested in building their own pyramids.

Most of us have seen a quarry. The Egyptian quarries looked very much the same, as we can see from the photograph on this page. Also the methods used in quarrying rock for building purposes have not changed so very much since the time of the ancient Egyptians. The main advantage that we have over the quarrymen in ancient Egypt lies in the quality of our tools. We have much harder metals, such as steel, which they did not possess. In fact they had to make do with copper, which is a soft metal and not very suitable for making into tools because copper tools soon become blunt with use. In spite of this they managed to quarry millions of tons of rock to build the pyramids and temples. This just goes to show what expert quarriers of stone the Egyptians must have been.

Ancient limestone quarry at Beni Hasan.

Some of these copper tools have been found by archaeologists, and we know from these discoveries that the ancient Egyptians could make very good copper tools, such as saws and chisels with which they could cut any kind of limestone. They

a Copper mortise chisel.
b Copper mason's chisel.
c Copper mason's chisel, New Kingdom, from Ghorab.
d Long copper quarryman's chisel, from Gebelein.
e Mason's mallet from Saqqara.
f Pounding-ball of dolerite from Aswan.
g Wedge for handling stone from Saqqara; traces of crushing are clearly shown.
h Believed to be a polishing tool, this black granite block of unknown date was found at Saqqara.
Note: these tools are not to scale.

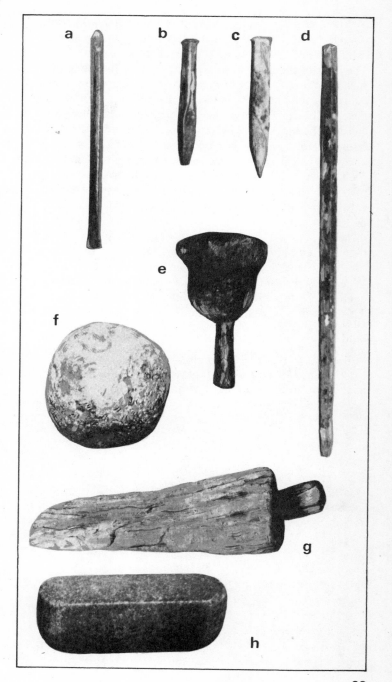

also used wedges and levers made of wood. Wood was a very precious material in Egypt where trees were very scarce. That is one of the reasons why stone, which is plentiful in Egypt, was used so much for building purposes. It also explains why they became so good at building in stone.

As we already know, the Egyptians worked different quarries to obtain the two different types of stone. They also had to use different methods, as it was a much more difficult job to quarry the hard granite than it was to quarry the much softer limestone.

The ancient Egyptians found that quarrying limestone was fairly easy. The poorer-quality limestone was obtained from the surface of the rock in the same way that some coal is taken from the surface by what is now called the open-cast method. This was by far the easiest way of quarrying limestone, so most of the limestone used in the centre or core of the pyramid was of this type. Fortunately this type of quarry was common in Egypt and also near to the pyramids. One example of such a quarry was at Giza where the Egyptians built the 'Great Pyramid' of Cheops, the pyramid of Chephren, the pyramid of Mycerinus and carved out the Sphinx.

A much better type of limestone was called Tura limestone after the place at which it was quarried. This was much farther up the Nile and the better quality stone could only be reached by mining. As we could have expected this stone was only used for special purposes such as forming the outside layer of the pyramid. It was like the icing on a Christmas cake. For show!

How did the Egyptians quarry their stone? We cannot say for certain, but by examining the tools used, the finished stones in the pyramids, and the unfinished stones in the quarries, we are able to describe how they might have done it.

When the Egyptians mined the limestone by means of tunnels, as at Tura, they first cut a hollow in the side of the cliff. This hollow had to be large enough for a man to work in. The floor of the hollow would be the top of the stone the men wished to quarry. A quarryman then crawled into this hollow and using long copper chisels cut down the back and sides of the stone block. They used wooden mallets to hammer down the chisels. The block would then be free on all sides except at the bottom. Holes would then be cut at the bottom of the block and wedges driven in to make the block split away from the rock to which it was joined. Sometimes the wedges were made of wood which swelled up when soaked with water, again causing the rock to split along the bottom. Great care had to be taken at this stage or the rock might have split in the wrong direction, ruining all their previous hard work. The block was then levered out of the way and work started on the next block of stone. This time the workmen had plenty of head-room. When they reached floor-level they would have to start all over again at the top and go farther into the cliff at the same time. This type of quarry left huge holes in the cliffs which can still be seen today.

Entrances to the ancient galleries in the limestone quarries at Ma'sara. A man may just be seen standing at the entrance to the central gallery.

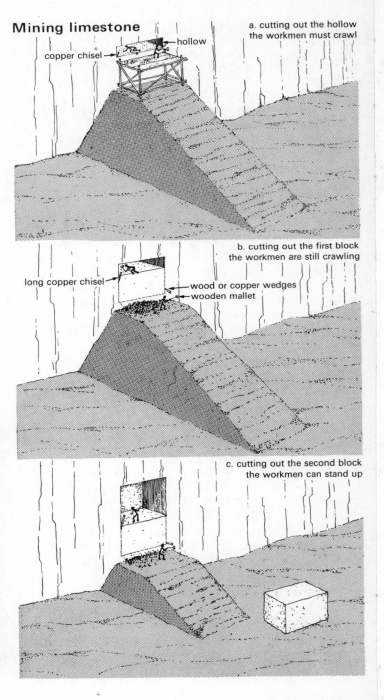

Mining limestone

copper chisel — hollow

a. cutting out the hollow the workmen must crawl

long copper chisel

wood or copper wedges
wooden mallet

b. cutting out the first block the workmen are still crawling

c. cutting out the second block the workmen can stand up

The end of one of the galleries at Ma'sara.

As we know open-cast quarrying was much easier than tunnel quarrying because the rock lay at the surface. They used the long chisels and the wedges exactly as they did for mining, but more men could work at once over a larger area of ground. Open-cast quarrying was therefore much quicker than mining. Copper saws were also used in quarrying but by far the most important tools were the chisel and the wedge.

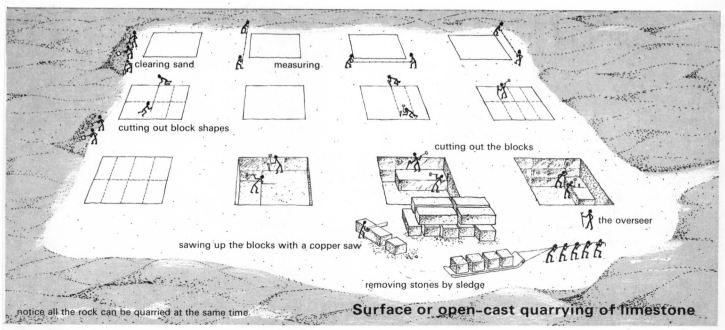

clearing sand   measuring

cutting out block shapes

cutting out the blocks

the overseer

sawing up the blocks with a copper saw

removing stones by sledge

notice all the rock can be quarried at the same time.

Surface or open-cast quarrying of limestone

Quarrying hard rocks, like granite, was much more difficult even than mining the Tura limestone. Also, the granite quarries were to be found hundreds of miles farther up the Nile, at a place called Aswan. Luckily not so much stone of this type was needed for the pyramids.

No tunnelling was done to obtain granite. If the better rock lay under several feet of poorer rock a fire was made on the top surface of the rock. When the rock became hot enough it started to crumble, and if the water was thrown on it the surface of the rock could be rubbed away in flakes. The Egyptians did this time and time again until they reached the better granite. They would then cut out the block they wanted by using their chisels and wedges as they did when quarrying limestone.

Some people think that they did not quarry granite at all when the pyramids were being built and could find all the granite they needed from loose blocks lying on the surface. They say that the copper tools would have been too easily blunted by the very hard granite. Others think that the Egyptians had discovered a special way which has now been forgotten of making copper harder. Like many things about ancient Egypt we do not know for certain which is the truth. We can only guess at the most reasonable solution.

Another method we are certain was used to quarry granite, was that they banged all around the block of stone they wanted with a ball of dolerite. This was a very hard, round green stone found near the Red Sea. This knocked the rock off in flakes and took a very long time. In fact any method used in quarrying granite must have taken a very long time indeed, and have meant much hard, patient work for the quarrymen. But in ancient Egypt time was of little concern! After all 'this was only the Egyptian's short mortal life, a preparation for an everlasting life after death'!

The first batch of stones would be ready for their journey to the site of the pyramid. The problem would then be to get them there; certainly no easy task! But where pyramids were concerned the Egyptians were used to solving problems. The next chapter describes how they solved this particular problem of transporting the stones from the quarries to the pyramids.

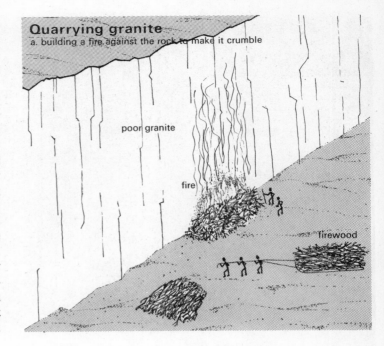

Quarrying granite
a. building a fire against the rock to make it crumble

poor granite

fire

firewood

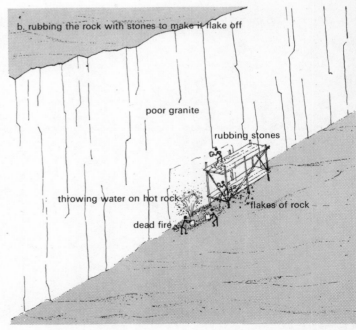

b. rubbing the rock with stones to make it flake off

poor granite

rubbing stones

throwing water on hot rock

flakes of rock

dead fire

above left: Quarrying at Aswan as it was still conducted well into this century.

above: A dolerite ball resting on an unfinished obelisk at Aswan.

c. cutting out the good granite with copper tools such as were used on the limestone

poor granite

wooden mallet

good granite

copper chisel

wood or copper wedges

dolerite balls

4. TRANSPORTING THE STONE

Boat building, showing tools used by the carpenters.

The steering paddle of a model boat, *c.* 2100 BC.

How did the ancient Egyptians move the stone from the quarries to the pyramid being built? As we know, the larger pyramids used up millions of tons of stone, most of which was in two-and-a-half-ton blocks. This was no easy task, yet the Egyptians managed to find a way.

If we look once again at the map of ancient Egypt on page 10, we can see how they did it. All the pyramids lie near the river and so do the old quarries. Taking Giza as an example, we can see that the poorer-quality limestone was near the pyramids; the Tura limestone at Tura farther up the Nile; and the granite at Aswan even farther up the river. The obvious solution was to carry the stone in boats down the river Nile.

Why not use the roads? There would be no roads as such; only tracks across the sandy desert. Also it is thought that when the pyramids were first built the Egyptians did not have the wheel. They had to use sledges, pulled by men. Think of all the men needed to move all those stones such great distances! Also, might not the heavily laden sledges sink into the soft sand of the desert? The river was the obvious way in which to transport the stone. This is true today of the Nile, which still carries a great deal of traffic.

Perhaps the best way in which to explain the transport of the pyramid stone is to describe the journey of a stone-carrying boat from the point of its departure at a pyramid site, to one of the quarries and back again.

There were probably two main types of boat, the large flat-bottomed barge used for carrying the great statues and obelisks, and the smaller, canoe-shaped boat used for more general purposes. Their basic equipment was however the same. They had a large square sail attached to a single mast in the centre of the boat. This was to take advantage of any wind which might arise, but it was not the main means of moving the boat. On either side of the boat was a row of oars which certainly had to be used when it was sailing down the Nile against the prevailing wind. At the rear of the boat was a large, paddle-shaped rudder which the helmsman used to steer the boat.

Although these boats were large, they were probably not seaworthy. The busiest 'highway' of Egypt has always been the Nile, and for this reason the ancient Egyptian sailor must surely have been, above all else, a natural river sailor.

A photograph taken in the 1950s showing a boy pulling on the oars of a Nile boat.

The ancient Egyptians did, however, build boats to sail on the open sea, for records of voyages on the Red Sea and the Mediterranean have come down to us. But they never became really good boat-builders because the few trees in Egypt were not really suitable for this purpose. Good wood had to be brought all the way from the Lebanon and was therefore rather difficult to obtain, and very expensive.

The boat would leave Giza for the quarry at Tura up-river. If there was a favourable breeze the sail would be hoisted but oarsmen would still have to row to make headway against the swollen river.

A Nile boat under full sail.

A sailor would beat out the time to a monotonous rhythm. They would row in time to this rhythm and probably chant out well-known songs at the same time. This helped them to put up with the hard, back-breaking work of rowing under the hot Egyptian sun. A foreman or overseer would be watching the rowers to see that they did not slack in their work. The man at the helm had a job which required both skill and knowledge of the river. If he made a mistake the boat could easily run aground on one of the many sandbanks in the Nile.

The boat would not be travelling empty up to the quarries at Tura. Fresh supplies of equipment and food for the workers at the quarry would be on board. Perhaps there would even be a new batch of workers to relieve the quarry gangs who had finished their tour of duty. Sometimes fresh instructions to the chief overseer at the quarry would be sent in the form of a papyrus roll. Sometimes, but more rarely perhaps, a government inspector would travel on the boat to see for himself how the quarrying was progressing.

At last the boat would reach Tura, unload its cargo of men and supplies, and prepare to load up again with its cargo of stones. But how were these large stones brought down to the river from the quarries, which were sometimes a mile away? By sledge, is the probable answer. What were these sledges like? They did not look so very different from the sledges used to slide down snow-clad hills. Like most of these sledges, they were also made of wood, but of course they had to be much bigger to hold such large blocks of stone. They did not have snow to slide down, so how did they move? The stone was first levered on to the sledge, probably from a ledge or ramp above it, and tied firmly on with ropes. Ropes were then attached to the front of the sledge and held by a gang of men who pulled the sledge along. Water or some other liquid was poured on the ground to help the sledge to slide along. The number of men needed to pull the sledge depended on the weight of the stone it carried, and as labour was plentiful this was no problem to the Egyptians. In fact, beasts of burden such as oxen were considered far too precious for such work.

The sledges would be pulled to the boat and the stones levered and dragged on board. This was no easy task because the Egyptians had no knowledge of the pulley, and therefore no lifting equipment. Some of the very large stones were probably left on the sledges to save time and trouble at the other end. I wonder how many of these fragile boats were

Transporting the stone

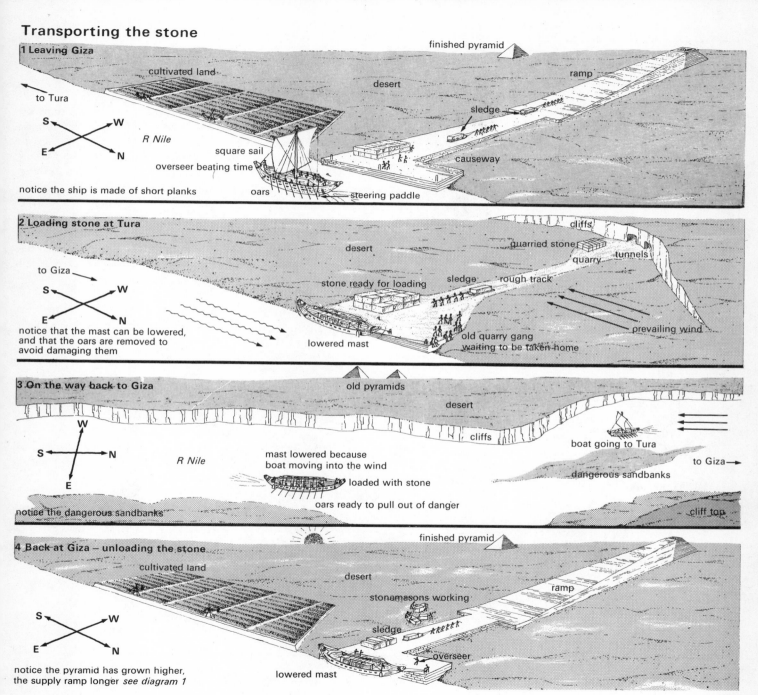

1 Leaving Giza

finished pyramid

cultivated land

desert

ramp

to Tura

S W E N

R Nile

square sail

overseer beating time

notice the ship is made of short planks

oars

steering paddle

sledge

causeway

2 Loading stone at Tura

cliffs

quarried stone

quarry

tunnels

desert

to Giza

S W E N

stone ready for loading

sledge

rough track

notice that the mast can be lowered, and that the oars are removed to avoid damaging them

lowered mast

old quarry gang waiting to be taken home

prevailing wind

3 On the way back to Giza

old pyramids

desert

W S N E

cliffs

boat going to Tura

R Nile

mast lowered because boat moving into the wind

to Giza →

dangerous sandbanks

loaded with stone

notice the dangerous sandbanks

oars ready to pull out of danger

cliff top

4 Back at Giza — unloading the stone

finished pyramid

cultivated land

desert

ramp

stonemasons working

S W E N

sledge

notice the pyramid has grown higher, the supply ramp longer *see diagram 1*

overseer

lowered mast

31

damaged during the loading and unloading of the stones? How many workers were crushed to death under toppling blocks of stone? A lot of men did die whilst working in the quarries. It would be interesting to know how many of these lost their lives whilst helping to load a boat.

At last, to the relief of all concerned, the boat would be loaded and ready to sail for Giza. As well as the stones, perhaps it also carried a returning quarry gang and the government inspector if he had completed his business. Even going down the river the oarsmen would be unable to rest, as the sail could not be raised because the wind would be blowing against them. Also the dangers were even greater than on the upward journey. Now the boat was heavily laden down with stone. If it struck a sandbank it would be virtually impossible to set it free again. The helmsman had to be doubly alert at his great steering-paddle, and the oarsmen had to be ready at all times to pull away at the slightest sign of danger.

left: Transporting a colossal statue, *c.* 1500 BC. Note the man pouring oil or water in front of the sledge to grease the skids.

above: The causeway to the pyramid of Unas at Saqqara.

left: Lowering the mast of a Nile boat.

At long last the journey would be over and the boat would pull into the side of the river nearest the pyramid site. At the river bank an overseer would be waiting with his gang to unload the boat. Once again the dangerous and difficult task of moving the heavy stones was repeated; this time from the boat to the shore.

When the boat had been unloaded the stones were taken to the pyramid on sledges. At the pyramid the stonemasons would be waiting to trim the stones to the correct shape and size for the builders.

Each pyramid had a causeway connecting it to the Nile. This was really just a road cut out of the rocks with walls on either side and a roof, apart from the two earliest which did not have a roof. The roof and walls of the causeway were not built until the pyramid was complete. The causeway was intended to serve eventually as a road for the funeral procession when it travelled from the river to the pyramid. It would be built at the same time that the pyramid site was being prepared. This was very convenient for the builders who could use the causeway as a good road for their sledges.

We can see then that transporting such large quantities of stone by both land and water was a difficult and often dangerous task. That the Egyptians overcame these difficulties says much for their skill, powers of organization, and most of all determination. We shall see in the next chapter how these qualities once again played a great part in the actual building of the pyramids.

5. THE BUILDING OF THE PYRAMID

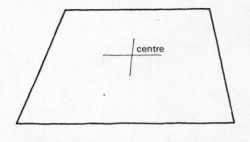

a. Having found the centre of the base, the stones are laid in the form of a square, working from the centre outwards.

The builders would now be ready to start the actual building of the pyramid. The huge square base of rock would be smooth and strong, waiting for the tremendous weight of the monument which it would have to support. The builder would have large supplies of stone already at the site, whilst more stones were being quarried and would be ready when they were needed.

The builders needed to remember two things whilst they were building the pyramid. They were first, that the pyramid must be strong all the way through, and secondly, that when it was finished it should look like a pyramid and nothing else. These points were obvious, because if it was not firm inside, the pyramid would collapse; and if the angles and sides were crooked people would laugh at it rather than admire it. We shall see later on how they checked to see that this did not happen.

As we learnt in chapter 4, the builders did not have the pulley, which is the easiest way of lifting large stones. They had to use wooden levers instead, but these on their own would be of little use as the pyramid grew higher. No person today can say for certain how the pyramids were actually built, but a great many people have made guesses from facts that we do know to be true. There are many of these theories, some possible and some just ridiculous. The method of building we are going to consider seems the most likely one to have been used by the Egyptians.

The builders took the blocks of stone on sledges to the centre of the square foundation. The stones were placed together so that they formed a small square inside the much larger square of the base. Stones were added to all sides of this small square

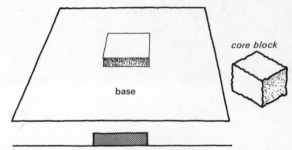

b. The workmen lay blocks of poorer local limestone. These are called *core blocks* because they lie at the centre of the pyramid.

A core block: notice that it has been cut only roughly. The bulk of the pyramid is composed of these blocks.

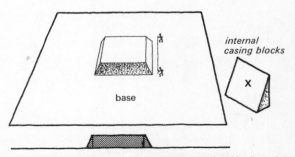

c. Better quality limestone is used when the shape of the first square needs correcting. Blocks of Tura limestone are used. These are called *internal casing blocks*.

An internal casing block: notice the way the stone has been cut. The side marked **X** faces outwards.

34

until it gradually grew larger and larger, but still kept the shape of a square. The stones used so far were only rough blocks. They were roughly cube-shaped like a rectangular sugar-lump, but not so smooth, apart from the top and bottom of each block which had to be smooth to stand steadily on the smooth, level base, and support the blocks above. If the bottoms of the blocks were not smooth they would wobble, causing other blocks in the pyramid to move, and perhaps the pyramid to collapse. These stones are called *core-blocks*.

As the core-blocks were rough and bumpy it became more and more difficult to keep this first layer, as we shall call it, in the form of a square. The builders then placed special blocks of stone made of Tura limestone around the square, and checked to see that it was indeed a perfect square. If it was not, they would move the blocks of Tura limestone until it became a perfect square. This was one of the checks we mentioned earlier: to make sure that the pyramid remained firm inside and kept its proper shape. The outer face of the Tura limestone block would be cut so as to incline inwards at an angle of about 75° but it would be left rough. This again helped to check the pyramid's shape and strength. These stones are called *internal-casing-blocks*.

The builders would then lay some more core-blocks exactly as before, until they needed to correct the square again. Once more the slanted internal-casing-blocks would be used for this purpose. This procedure was repeated at regular intervals until the square of the first layer was almost as big as the square base. Only a narrow margin of the base would remain visible.

Before this stage the builders had not worried about fitting the stones together too carefully. But it was really important that the next row of stones around the square were fitted together as closely as possible. These stones are called *packing-blocks*. The builders could then say that they had finished the core, or inside of the square, and had only to put on the outer-casing, or shell of the first layer.

Now was the time for the builders to be really careful, because the stones they were now going to put into position made up the outside of the pyramid. These stones could be seen and could make or mar the appearance of the pyramid. Only the best quality limestone was used for these stones. These casing-stones were often fitted together on the ground to make sure they fitted tightly together when placed in their correct position in the pyramid.

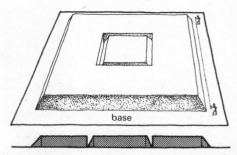

d. Alternate borders of core blocks and internal casing blocks are laid round the first square. Every time the internal casing blocks are used the square is measured, to ensure that it remains a perfect square. Only two borders of the internal casing blocks are shown here: the number varies in different pyramids.

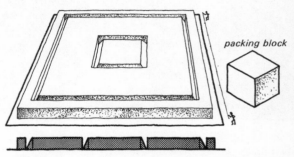

e. The last but one row of stones to be laid is made up of *packing blocks*, again of local limestone. They must fit together closely and form the outside of a perfect square.

A packing block: usually of local limestone, but unlike the core block it must be cut very carefully so that each block fits snugly.

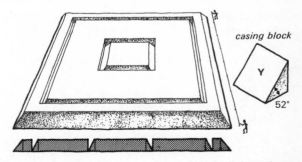

f. The final row of stones laid are called *casing blocks*. Made of best quality Tura limestone, they form the 'skin' of the pyramid and must fit together perfectly. A last check is made to see that a square has been perfectly maintained.

A casing block: all the surfaces are made smooth except the sloping side marked **Y**. This side slopes at the same angle as the intended pyramid.

The pyramid of Cheops, showing packing blocks. These stones would not be visible in an undamaged pyramid.

Casing blocks on the north side of the Great Pyramid. Notice the exposed packing blocks behind the casing blocks.

The bottoms of the stones which would rest on the base, both sides of the stones which rested against other casing-stones, and the backs of the stones which rested against the packing-blocks, had to be made perfectly smooth. The front surfaces of the packing-blocks would already have been made smooth. The front sides of the casing-blocks would be cut roughly to the same angle as the pyramid.

Before these blocks were laid the builders spread a thin layer of mortar on the stones into which a casing-block would fit. The sledge then brought the stone up and it was carefully levered into position, the watery mortar helping it to slip tightly into place. Probably it would sometimes have been necessary to coax it into position by men hauling on ropes and using wooden levers. This was a tricky job as some of these blocks weighed more than ten tons and needed to be laid perfectly, if the pyramid was to be a success. When the final casing-block had been wedged in on the first square or layer, it was time for the builders to check once again that it still

formed a perfect square. This was particularly important lower down the pyramid, as a very small error at the bottom could grow into a very large error by the time the top was reached. We can see this for ourselves in any sum where we make a small mistake at the beginning and reach an answer that is hopelessly wrong. So we can see that the pyramid-builders needed to be very careful in their work.

The builders then started on the next layer of the pyramid using exactly the same methods and checks as they did for the first layer. The only difference this time was that, as the first square of stones was slightly smaller than the square forming the base, so the second layer would be smaller than the first layer. Each layer would be a smaller square than the one on which it stood, leading to a very small square at the top of the pyramid. The top of each layer had to be made smooth in readiness for the next layer.

All four sides of the pyramid would slope upwards and inwards at the same angle, and meet at the four sides of the little

The pyramid of Chephren viewed from the summit of the Great Pyramid.

square at the top. The capstone, which is like a tiny pyramid made of granite, was fixed on the top of the square and jointed firmly into place.

Now all the builders had to do was smooth down each face of the pyramid so that it would be a tomb worthy of their great king. But wait a moment! Perhaps we should ask ourselves a few questions before we go any further.

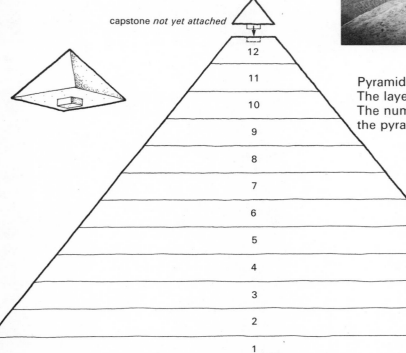

capstone *not yet attached*

12
11
10
9
8
7
6
5
4
3
2
1

Pyramid section showing numbered layers or squares. The layers are numbered to show the order of building. The number of layers varied according to the size of the pyramid.

The pyramid is very high and steep. How did the builders get so high? How could they hang on to its steeply sloping sides? How did they get those heavy stones higher than the first layer using only levers? The answer is of course that they did not use levers alone, but probably made use of a supply ramp and foothold embankments.

The supply ramp was made up of bricks and earth, and, as its name suggests, it was a road upon which the stones were taken up to the pyramid. A layer of earth and bricks was placed along the whole of one side of the pyramid when the first layer or square had been laid down. If the first layer was ten feet high then the end of the ramp touching the side of the pyramid must also have been ten feet high for about forty feet away from the pyramid. This was to give the builders room in which to move the stones being laid at the edge of the pyramid. The ramp then sloped gently away until it reached ground level.

As the pyramid rose, so the ramp rose also, and it became longer and longer before it reached ground level. The reason for this is obvious. If the ramp rose higher but remained the same length, it would become much steeper, and the builders would find it impossible to drag up the heavy stones on sledges. These ramps probably had a gradient of 1 in 12. This means that for every one foot the ramp rose in height it stretched twelve feet in length. This gradient of 1 in 12 would remain the same until the top of the pyramid was finished. Is there a hill of 1 in 12 in your district? If there is, go and look at it to see how steep it is.

As the sides of the pyramid began to slope upwards and inwards so the sides of the ramp had to slope at the same angle upwards and inwards in order to remain steady. The surface of the ramp was paved with wooden logs over which water could be poured to make the sledges run more smoothly.

Side view of a supply ramp during three stages of construction

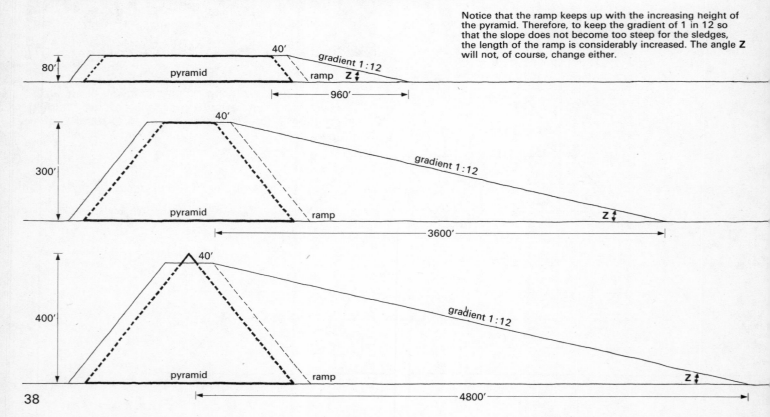

Notice that the ramp keeps up with the increasing height of the pyramid. Therefore, to keep the gradient of 1 in 12 so that the slope does not become too steep for the sledges, the length of the ramp is considerably increased. The angle **Z** will not, of course, change either.

The foothold embankments were almost exactly the same as the supply ramp except that they were much steeper and only had logs on the flat top of the embankment. They covered the other three sides of the pyramid and together with the supply ramp formed a sort of road forty feet wide, all round the level of the pyramid upon which the builders were working.

As the pyramid rose so did the foothold embankments and the supply ramp. At no time during building would the actual pyramid be visible. After the capstone was put on the top of the pyramid the workmen would begin to smooth and polish the pyramid from top to bottom. From top to bottom is actually true. They started with the capstone and worked down to the bottom of the pyramid.

The masons' labourers removed the brick and earth of the supply ramp and embankments as the masons worked down the pyramid. When the masons wanted to finish the job more quickly the labourers probably removed more earth at once and put up scaffolding as we do on modern buildings. This would make it possible for more men to work on the face of the pyramid at any one time.

Finally we need the answer to one more question. How did the Egyptians manage to build the corridors and rooms in their pyramid? As we know, most of the pyramid is solid and it rests on solid rock. The rooms and corridors underground had to be cut out of the solid rock. The rooms and corridors of the pyramid itself had to be put in whilst the pyramid was being built. The stones used were usually best-quality limestone, granite and other hard rocks.

The builders decided on which level they wanted a room and what its size was going to be. The stones were then probably cut to size on the ground, and often put together and numbered before being sent up the pyramid. There they would be very

A pyramid under construction, showing the supply ramp and the foothold embankments

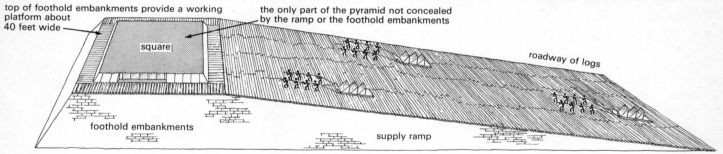

top of foothold embankments provide a working platform about 40 feet wide

the only part of the pyramid not concealed by the ramp or the foothold embankments

square

roadway of logs

foothold embankments

supply ramp

Smoothing down the faces of the pyramid

With the capstone in place the actual building of the pyramid is completed. The faces of the pyramid are smoothed while the supply ramp and embankments are gradually removed. Working from scaffolding, a large area can be smoothed at any one time.

exposed pyramid

scaffolding

roadway of logs no longer needed

bricks and earth

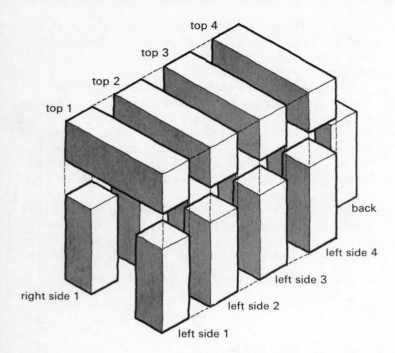

top 4
top 3
top 2
top 1

back

left side 4

left side 3

left side 2

left side 1

right side 1

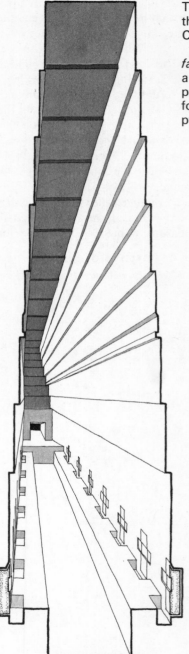

The Grand Gallery in the Great Pyramid of Cheops.

far left: Constructing a room. The various parts were marked for reassembly in the pyramid.

carefully put together again, rather like a jig-saw puzzle, using the numbers as a check. The squares or layers would be built up around the rooms and corridors. The corridors and rooms had to be well built because thousands of tons of stone would be resting on their roofs. The entrance to the pyramid was made in the same way, and it was impossible to enter a pyramid until the embankments and supply ramp had been removed from the faces of the pyramid.

We must remember that the building of the actual pyramid, its rooms, corridors, supply ramp and foothold embankments, was all done at the same time. Look again at the pictures and diagrams, try to imagine the pyramid growing stage by stage, and you will see how great an achievement it was for the Egyptians to have built the pyramids so long ago.

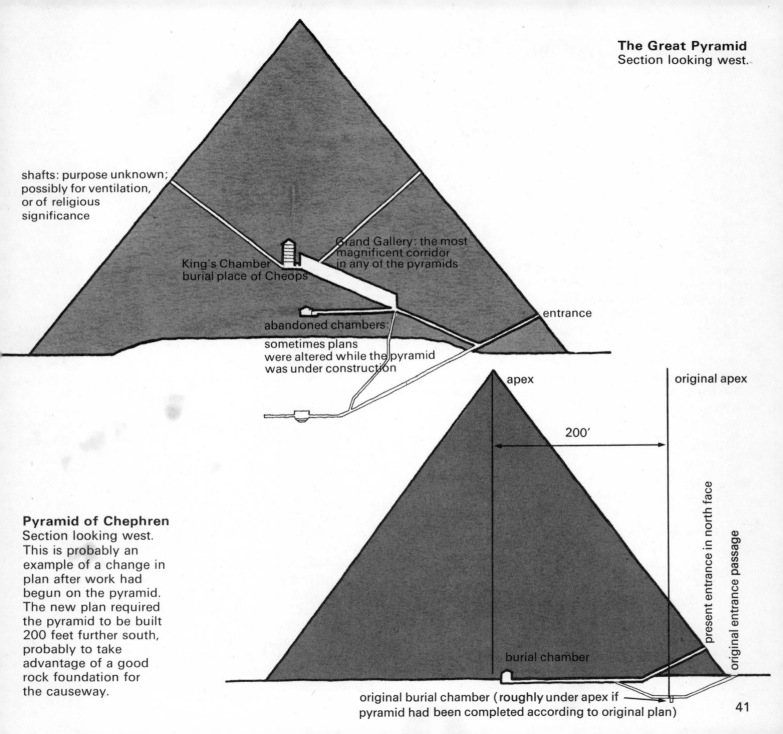

The Great Pyramid
Section looking west.

shafts: purpose unknown;
possibly for ventilation,
or of religious
significance

Grand Gallery: the most
magnificent corridor
in any of the pyramids

King's Chamber
burial place of Cheops

abandoned chambers:

sometimes plans
were altered while the pyramid
was under construction

entrance

apex

original apex

200'

present entrance in north face

original entrance passage

Pyramid of Chephren
Section looking west.
This is probably an
example of a change in
plan after work had
begun on the pyramid.
The new plan required
the pyramid to be built
200 feet further south,
probably to take
advantage of a good
rock foundation for
the causeway.

burial chamber

original burial chamber (**roughly** under apex if
pyramid had been completed according to original plan)

41

6. THE WORKMEN OF THE PYRAMID AGE

Slaves struggling to move huge blocks of stone, their bare backs cut and bruised by the overseers' whips! That is the picture which comes to most people's minds when they think of the pyramids. Is this a true picture? The answer must be 'No'. It is possible that some slaves did help to build the pyramids, but unlikely, because there is very little evidence of slave labour in Egypt. In this chapter we shall examine each stage in the building of a pyramid and consider the sort of qualities or skills needed by the men who worked on a pyramid.

Pyramid-building can be divided into five different stages all of which required special qualities in the men concerned with each stage. These stages were:

(1) Planning the building, and surveying the site of the pyramid.

(2) Quarrying the stones.

(3) Shaping and carving the stones.

(4) Transporting the stones by land and water.

(5) Building the actual pyramid.

It is obvious that unskilled slaves, even whipped along to work, could not carry out any of these tasks by themselves. Neither could unskilled freemen. Even the transport of the stones needed a certain amount of skill and direction. There had of course, to be a great number of unskilled labourers to do the jobs which only needed pure physical effort: jobs like dragging the heavy sledges and levering the stones from one position to another. In a big shipyard or factory today many labourers are employed to do similar types of work.

If the labourers were not slaves, then where did they come from? Remember how in the second chapter we talked of the flooding of the river Nile. During the time from July to October when their land was flooded the Nile farmers had little to do. What better time in which to use them as labourers on the pyramid? The pharaoh also used his sailors and soldiers to collect stone from the quarries.

As we have already stated, all other work, apart from labouring, needed some kind of special skill. We shall now examine the skills needed by the different workers and compare them with the skills needed by similar workmen today.

The Egyptian surveyors and planners needed to be very intelligent men and had to be specially trained for their jobs. The Egyptian planner was like a modern architect. He had to imagine what the building would be like when it was built. He had to put his ideas down on papyrus in the form of a plan which would explain to the builder just what size the building should be, and what it should look like when it was finished.

The Egyptian surveyor was like our modern surveyor. He had to survey the site for building. He did this by measuring in various ways to make sure that it was suitable for such a building. This meant that he had to have a good knowledge of mathematics and know how to calculate directions by the stars. The surveyor put into practice the first stages of the planner's ideas.

I am a pharaoh.
I need a pyramid for
my life after death.
My body shall lie
in the pyramid, together
with my goods and most
treasured possessions.

 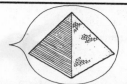

We are a modern family.
We want a house for
this life, and we hope
our friends will come
to visit us. Usually
houses are built of
bricks, but we want
ours of stone.

I am the architect.
I make a plan of the
pyramid on a papyrus
roll.

I am the architect.
I shall make a plan
of the house at my
drawing board.

I am the surveyor.
I find a good site for
the pyramid, and measure
the foundations. I check
my measurements against
the architect's plans.

I am the surveyor.
I check that the site
is suitable for building
on, and measure the
foundations. I check my
measurements against
the architect's plans.

 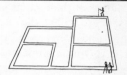

I am the overseer at a
quarry. I see that the men
work hard and quarry
the stone in the correct
manner.

I am the foreman at a
quarry. I see that the men
work hard, and quarry
the stone in the correct
manner.

I am the overseer of
the stone-masons. I
make sure they cut and
shape the stones correctly.

I am the foreman of
the stone-masons. I
make sure they cut and
shape the stones correctly.

I am the overseer of
the men who move the stone
to where it is needed.
On land we use sledges . . .
On the river we use boats . . .

I am a lorry driver.
I transport the stone
on my lorry to where
it is needed.

I am the overseer of the
men who build the pyramid.
My job is to see that the
pyramid is well built.

I am the foreman of
the men who build the
house. My job is to
see that the house is
well built.

The Egyptian quarryman needed a great deal of practical skill. Not only did he have to use his hands cleverly but he also needed to gain a great deal of experience in his work before he could do some of the more difficult jobs. He had to know which methods and tools to use on the different types of rocks; how to cut out huge chunks of rock without their cracking; where to find the best rock and how to mine it. He was very little different from the modern quarryman except that he did not use explosives. The quarrymen worked in gangs and they probably had to mine a certain amount of stone during a regular period of time, such as a month. They painted the names of their gangs in red ochre on the stones. Some of the gangs were called the 'Boat Gang', 'South Gang', 'Enduring Gang', and there were others.

The Egyptian stonemason was a very skilled man. He was a very clever worker in stone, especially as we must realize that he had only copper tools. His work, which ranged from cutting sharp edges and smoothing blocks of stone, to very difficult carving in stone, is the equal of any work done by the modern stonemason.

Men were needed to make sure the stones were carried by land and river from the quarries to the pyramid. This meant men who were good at organizing other men. We could compare these men to the modern-day foreman in a large goods yard. The ancient Egyptian's difficulties were far greater than those of our foreman. Look back at the chapter on transport and you will realize that it was no easy job to see that these large blocks of stone reached their destination on time and in good condition. This was especially true on the river, where the sailors needed to be very careful in the navigation of their heavily laden boats on the swollen river.

The Egyptian builder could be compared with the modern bricklayer yet on a much grander scale. He had to lay blocks weighing from 2½ to 50 tons compared to the bricklayers' bricks of only a few pounds. When you consider that the Egyptians had neither modern lifting tackle such as cranes, nor special materials such as steel and pre-cast concrete, their achievement is all the more remarkable. The modern bricklayer gets very high wages, because he is a skilled man at his job. Surely his ancient Egyptian counterpart must have been equally, if not more, skilled at his work?

That such skilled men worked on the pyramids there is no doubt. It is also fairly certain that they were permanently employed on a pyramid until it was finished. Near the 'Great Pyramid' barracks or lodgings for 4,000 men have been unearthed. It is believed, from tools found on the spot, that this is where the builders and stonemasons lived whilst working on the pyramid. Great piles of stone chippings also help to show that the stonemason worked a great deal near the pyramid itself.

The greater number of men working on the pyramid were unskilled labourers. Most of these labourers were employed in moving the blocks of stone to wherever they were needed.

Quarry face at Ma'sara. The stone at the top has been cut away to start a new series of blocks.

It is probable that they only worked on the pyramid for the three months during the flood period and worked on the land for the remaining nine months of the year. The much smaller group of skilled workers would be employed permanently near the pyramid, or in the quarries. The planners and surveyors would be important men, probably always at the beck and call of the pharaoh.

When we think about the pyramid-builders we must not assume that because they lived such a long time ago that they must be very different from modern builders. The point to remember is that the pyramids were planned by architects and surveyors and built by the builders and their labourers. In exactly the same way the modern builder erects his small modern house, or tall block of flats. The amazing thing is that, using mainly man-power, the ancient Egyptian workmen could produce such a magnificent and lasting building as a pyramid. Let us ask ourselves just one question. How many modern buildings will last as long as the pyramids? I think we all know the answer.

Imhotep: the man who planned the Step Pyramid for King Zoser. He is also reputed to have been a magician, astronomer and the 'father of medicine'.

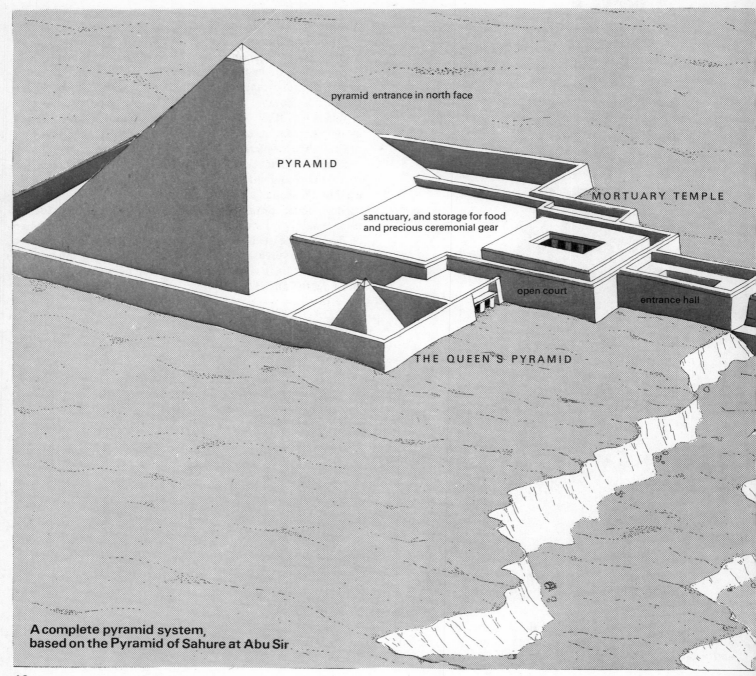

pyramid entrance in north face

PYRAMID

MORTUARY TEMPLE

sanctuary, and storage for food
and precious ceremonial gear

open court

entrance hall

THE QUEEN'S PYRAMID

A complete pyramid system,
based on the Pyramid of Sahure at Abu Sir

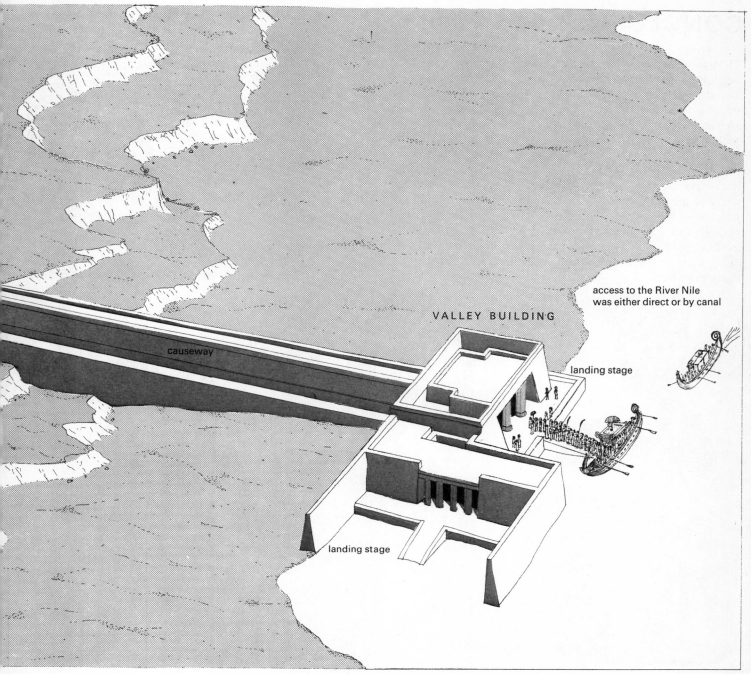

access to the River Nile
was either direct or by canal

VALLEY BUILDING

landing stage

causeway

landing stage

CONCLUSION

The pyramids are no longer white, gleaming and perfect as they were when first built thousands of years ago. For all their size and strength the pyramids failed to safeguard the bodies of the pharaohs and all were empty when examined by modern archaeologists. The tombs had been robbed centuries before; probably within a few hundred years of the building of the pyramids.

Today the pyramids stand battered and empty, but still impressive in their size and grandeur. They have outlasted many of the more recent works of man, and seem to fulfil the purpose of their builders, that they would last 'forever'. The pyramids are a reminder of a once great and civilized race who lived in the Nile Valley. In this lies their real importance. They did not guarantee the pharaohs everlasting life, but they do stand as monuments to the genius of their people.

Below are four pharaohs who were buried in the pyramids.

Mycerinus and his queen Chamerenebti (Giza).

Cheops (Giza).

Chephren (Giza).

Zoser (Saqqara).